AF575353

American Sign Language

Work

by E. Russell Primm III • illustrated by Kathleen Petelinsek

childsworld.com

Published by The Child's World®
800-599-READ • childsworld.com

Photography Credits
George Dolgikh/Shutterstock.com, cover; Prostock-studio/Shutterstock.com, 1, 8; SpeedKingz/Shutterstock.com, 3; Pressmaster/Shutterstock.com, 4, 6; EvgeniiAnd/Shutterstock.com, 5; PeopleImages.com–Yuri A/Shutterstock.com, 7; Rawpixel.com/Shutterstock.com, 9; YAKOBCHUK VIACHESLAV/Shutterstock.com, 10; Zoran Zeremski/Shutterstock.com, 11; Toa55/Shutterstock.com, 12; Gorodenkoff/Shutterstock.com, 13; Ground Picture/Shutterstock.com, 14; wavebreakmedia/Shutterstock.com, 15, 20; Studio Romantic/Shutterstock.com, 16; Fotokostic/Shutterstock.com, 17 ; Svitlana Hulko/Shutterstock.com, 18; pio3/Shutterstock.com, 19; Drazen Zigic/Shutterstock.com, 21

ISBN Information
9781503889088 (Reinforced Library Binding)
9781503890169 (Portable Document Format)
9781503891401 (Online Multi-user eBook)
9781503892644 (Electronic Publication)

LCCN 2023950376

Printed in the United States of America

Note to Parents, Caregivers, and Educators: The understanding of any language begins with the acquisition of vocabulary, whether the language is spoken or manual. The books in this series provide readers, both young and old, with basic American Sign Language signs. Combining close photo cues and simple, but detailed, line illustrations, children and adults alike can begin the process of learning American Sign Language.

Let these books be an introduction to the world of American Sign Language. Most languages have regional dialects and multiple ways of expressing the same thought. This is also true for sign language. We have attempted to use the most common version of the signs for the words in this series. As with any language, the best way to learn is to be taught in person by a frequent user. It is our hope that this series will pique your interest in sign language.

A special thanks to our advisers: As a member of a deaf family that spans four generations, **Kim Bianco Majeri** lives, works, and plays among the Deaf community. **Carmine L. Vozzolo** is an educator of children who are deaf and hard of hearing, as well as their families.

E. Russell Primm III was a well-known figure in the publishing industry who produced thousands of acclaimed books for children. He was affiliated with organizations such as the American Library Association, the Chicago Book Clinic, and the University of Chicago Publishing Program Advisory Board.

Kathleen Petelinsek has loved books since she was a child. Through the years, she has written, designed, and illustrated many books for children. She lives in Wisconsin, near her granddaughter who also shares her love for books.

Actors often go to special classes to learn their job.

Actor

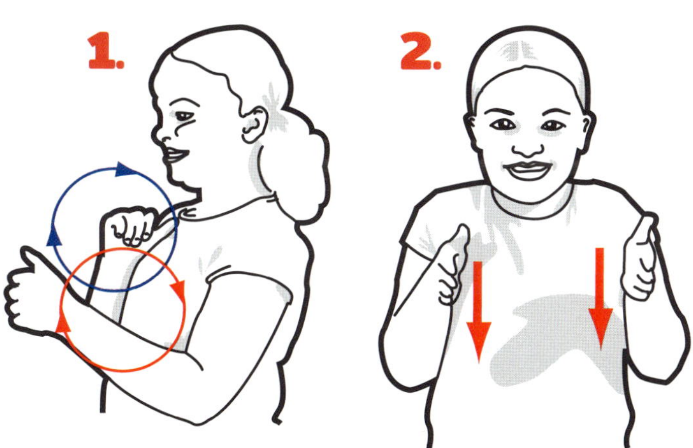

Make the letter "A" with both hands and rotate in front of your chest. Your thumbs brush your chest as they go by. Then face your palms together and move downward.

Artists work with everything from pencils and crayons to paint and plaster.

Artist

Make the letter "I" and move your pinky in a squiggly line down your left hand. Then face your palms together and move downward.

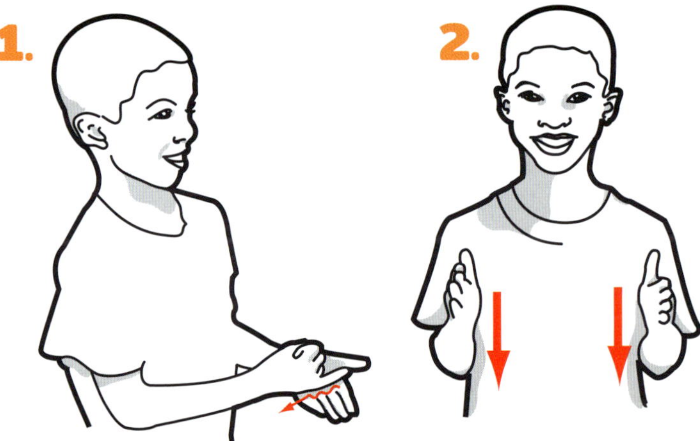

Carpenters know how to build and fix many types of wood and plastic.

Carpenter

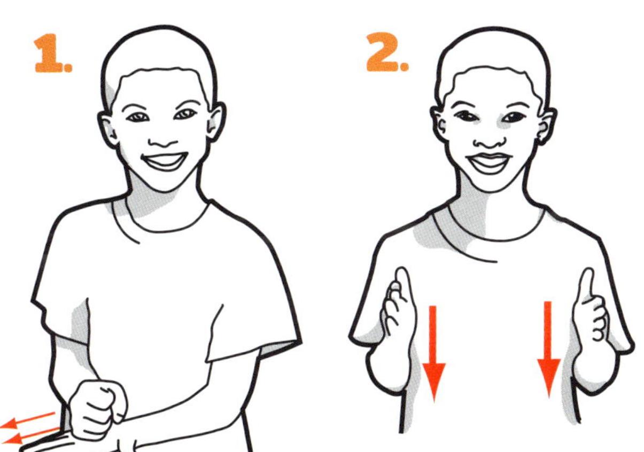

Slide your right fist over your left palm. Then face your palms together and move downward.

Cashiers work in stores, restaurants, gas stations, and many other places.

Cashier

Wiggle your fingers as if you are using a cash register. Then face your palms together and move downward.

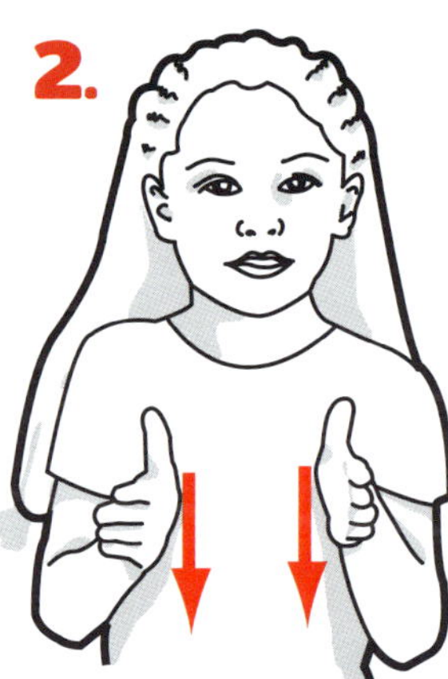

Many coaches volunteer. Others coach as their job.

Coach

Your right hand makes the letter "C" and taps your right shoulder twice.

Do you like to cook? Cooks often go to culinary school to learn their job.

Cook

Flip your right hand from palm-down to palm-up. Then face your palms together and move downward.

1.

2.

3.

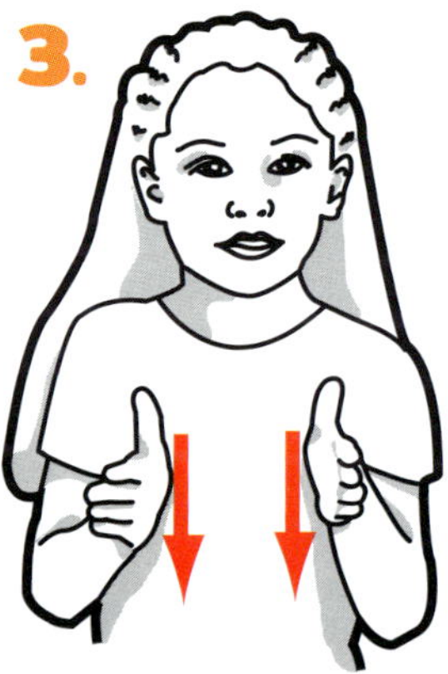

Dancers must be healthy and strong.

Dancer

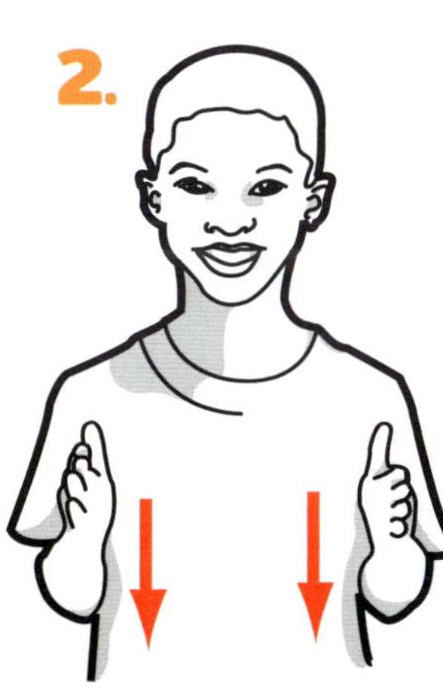

Make the letter "V" and swing back and forth over your left hand. Then face your palms together and move downward.

A doctor who treats children is called a pediatrician.

Doctor

Your right hand taps your left wrist twice.

Some farmers work on small farms. Others work for big companies.

Farmer

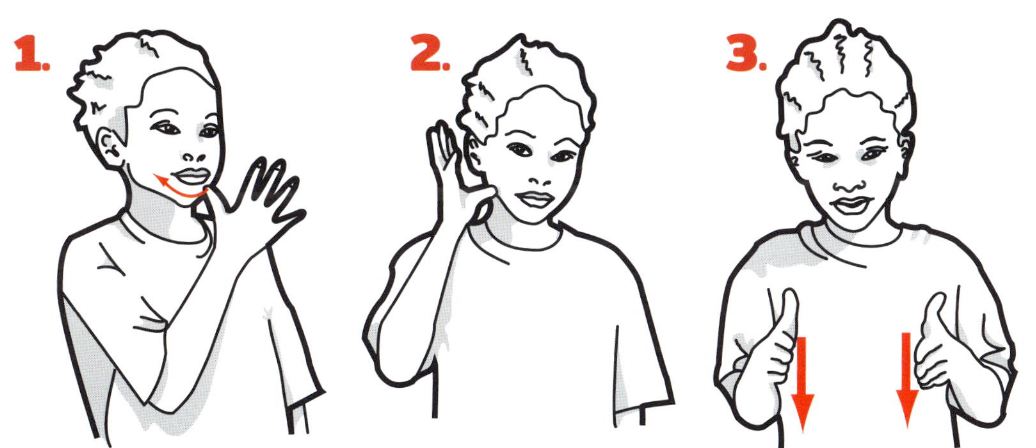

Your open right hand moves from the left side of your chin to the right side. Then face your palms together and move downward.

Firefighters must know how to stay calm in emergencies.

Firefighter

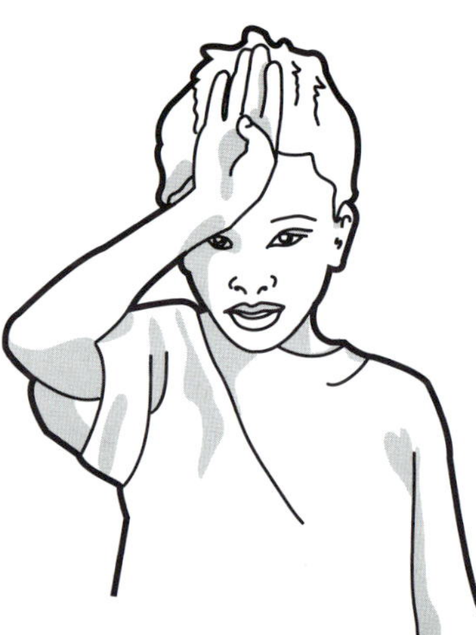

Your flat right hand taps your forehead twice.

A judge must be a good listener. Judges know how to apply the law to different situations.

Judge

Pretend you are banging a gavel.

Lawyers must be good at speaking and writing.

Lawyer

Make the letter "L." Bump your fist against your flat left hand twice. Then face your palms together and move downward.

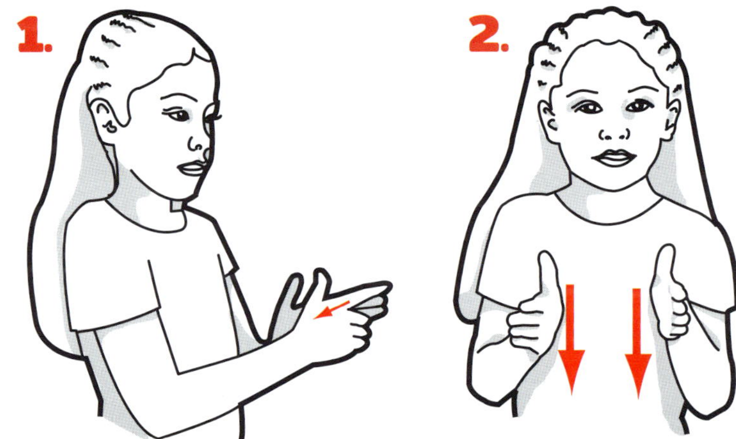

Librarians work at public libraries, schools, and many other places.

Librarian

Make the "L" shape. Circle around clockwise. Sometimes this sign finishes by facing your palms together and moving downward.

Nurses work everywhere from hospitals to schools.

Nurse

Your right hand makes the letter "N" and taps your left wrist twice.

Painters work on small houses and big buildings.

Painter

1.

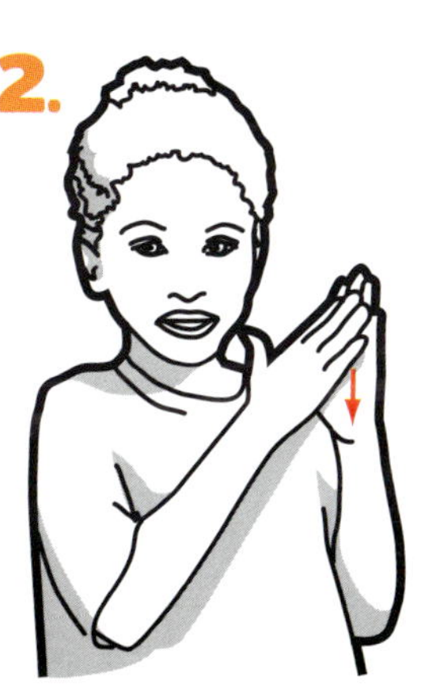
2.

3.

Move your right hand up and down against your left hand as if you were using a paintbrush. Then face your palms together and move downward.

Pilots fly everything from jets to helicopters.

Pilot

Bend your middle and ring fingers. "Fly" your hand forward. Then face your palms together and move downward.

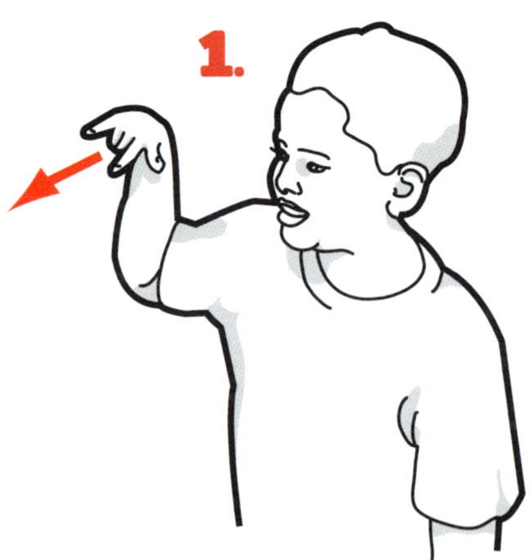

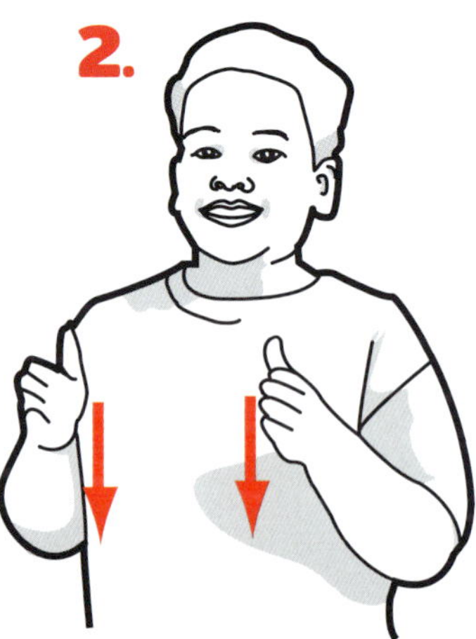

Police officers sometimes work very long hours.

Police Officer

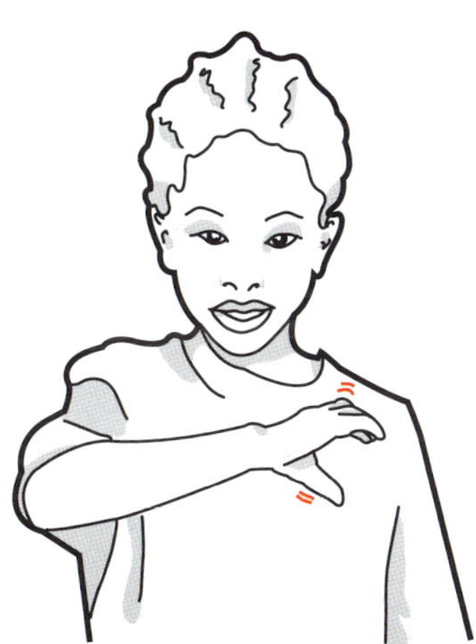

Your right hand makes the letter "C" and taps your upper left chest like a police badge.

Soldiers must be brave and in good shape. They need to complete difficult training.

Soldier

Both of your hands make the letter "A." Your right hand taps your chest twice while your left hand taps your ribs twice.

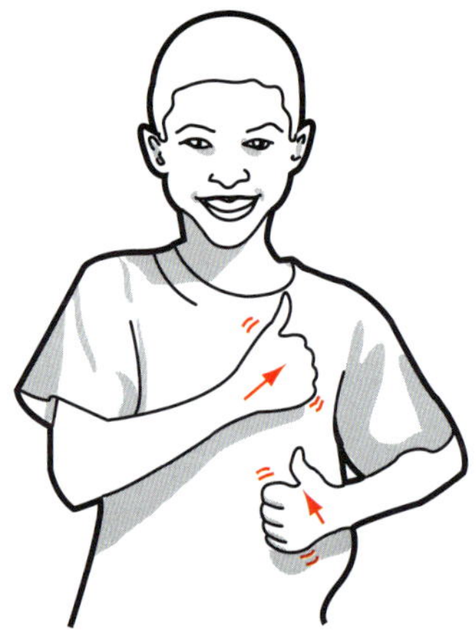

Teachers are caring and hardworking. They must know how to do many things at once.

Teacher

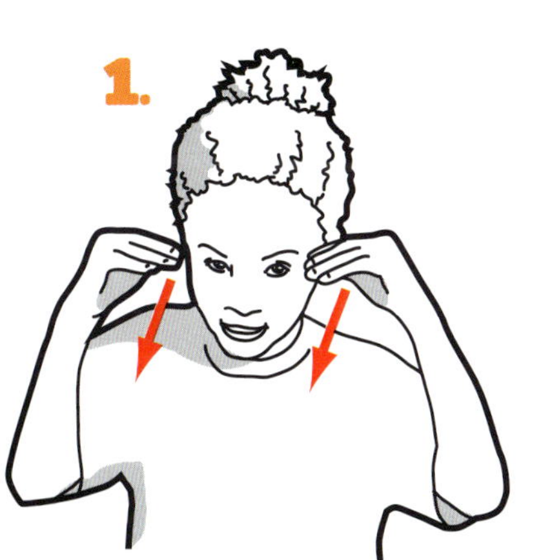

Move your hands outward, away from your forehead. Then face your palms together and move downward.

Wonder More

- How much did you know about American Sign Language (ASL) before reading this book? Do you already know some ASL signs? What new signs did you learn?

- Some words or specific names don't have signs. In these cases, you can spell the individual letters of the word, which is called fingerspelling. Look at the alphabet chart on page 23. Can you sign the letters in your name?

- With a partner, pick three signs from this book and practice them together. Are you able to understand each other? Is ASL easier or harder than you thought it would be?

- Think of a type of work or job that isn't in this book. Try spelling out the word with fingerspelling. Then look up the ASL sign for the word. Where can you find more ASL signs?

Sign Language Alphabet

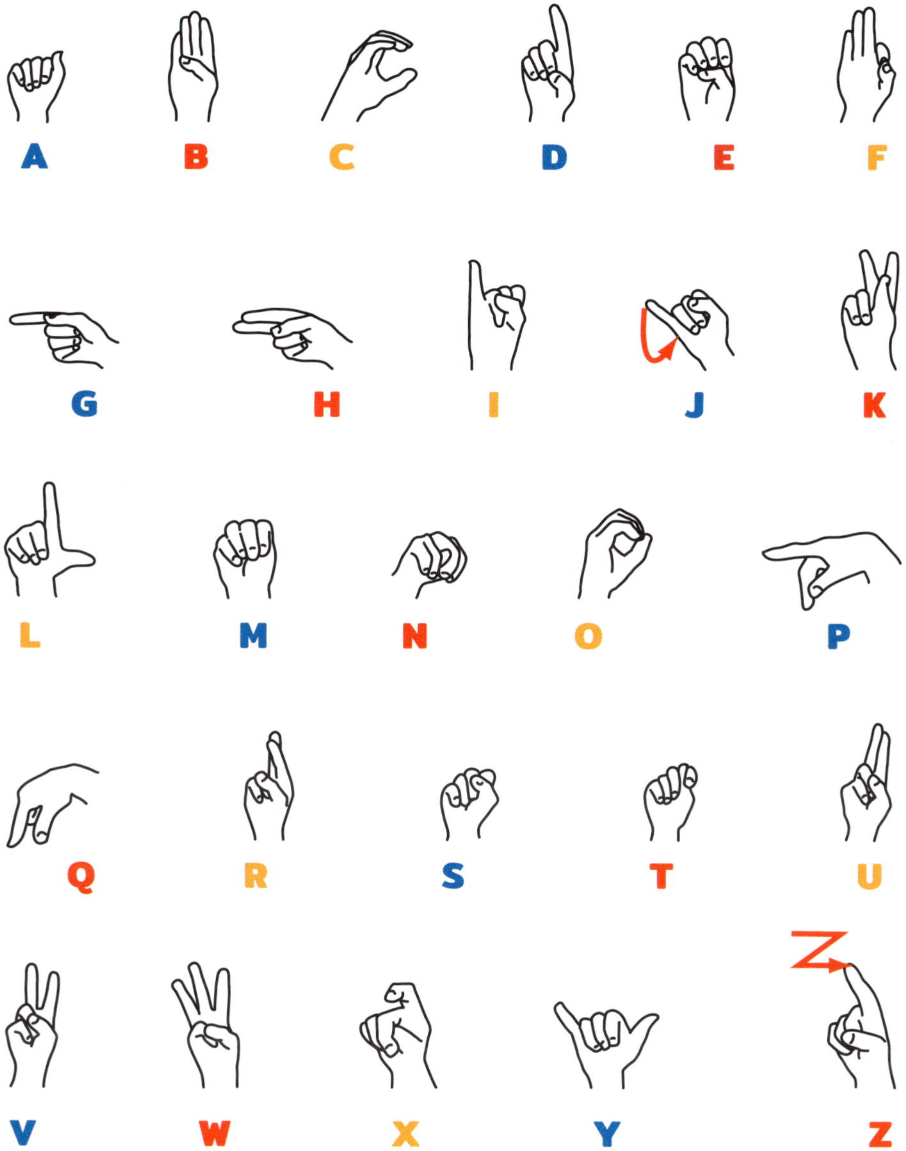

A B C D E F

G H I J K

L M N O P

Q R S T U

V W X Y Z

Find Out More

In the Library

Adams, Tara, and Natalia Sanabria (illustrator). *We Can Sign! An Essential Guide to American Sign Language for Kids*. Emeryville, CA: Rockridge Press, 2020.

Brakenhoff, Kelly, and Theresa Murray (illustrator). *Never Mind!* (Duke the Deaf Dog ASL Series). Lincoln, NE: Emerald Prairie Press, 2019.

On the Web

Visit our website for links about American Sign Language:
childsworld.com/links

Note to Parents, Caregivers, Teachers, and Librarians: We routinely verify our web links to make sure they are safe and active sites. So encourage your readers to check them out!

A Special Thank-You!

Thank you to our models from the Program for Children Who are Deaf and Hard of Hearing at the Alexander Graham Bell School in Chicago, Illinois.

Alina's favorite things to do are art, soccer, and swimming. DJ is her brother!

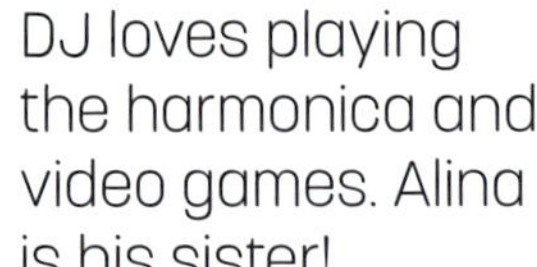

DJ loves playing the harmonica and video games. Alina is his sister!

Dareous likes football. His favorite team is the Detroit Lions. He also likes to play video games.

Jasmine likes writing and math in school. She also loves to swim.

Darionna likes the swings and merry-go-round on the playground. She also loves art.